Original title:
The Fern's Lament

Copyright © 2025 Creative Arts Management OÜ
All rights reserved.

Author: Jude Lancaster
ISBN HARDBACK: 978-1-80581-764-2
ISBN PAPERBACK: 978-1-80581-291-3
ISBN EBOOK: 978-1-80581-764-2

In the Heart of the Unearthed

Beneath the soil, a giggle grew,
With roots that danced in the morning dew.
They whispered secrets, oh so bright,
Of trowels lost in garden fright.

Worms wear hats and lead the choir,
Composing tunes that never tire.
Every worm wants a part to play,
In the fun beneath the leafy sway.

When the Sunlight Falters

In cloudy days, the shadows cuddle,
While leaves conspire in quiet huddle.
They tell of sunbeams and their tricks,
And how to dodge those pesky pricks.

A sunbeam slipped, a clumsy tease,
Fell in the grass, lost its keys.
Yet giggles echo, hearts could swell,
With tales of mishaps they know so well.

Fading Memories in Green

Once a sprout, a daring sprig,
Swore to grow tall, it danced a jig.
But now it bends, with pouting leaves,
Recalling days of summer thieves.

A blustering breeze, a playful tease,
Whispers of tales held in deep trees.
With each sway, a chuckle spills,
At memories lost among the frills.

Veil of the Whispering Woods

In the woods, where tall tales sway,
Foliage chuckles in a merry way.
Leaves knit gossip, light as air,
About the antics of passing bears.

Branches sway, with playful grace,
Telling stories of a silly race.
Among the ferns, laughter blooms,
As woodland critters share their dooms.

A Sigh Among the Stalks

In the garden, whispers fly,
Where leafy friends just sigh.
"Oh please, don't play that tune!"
Said a leaf under the moon.

With roots that twist and twine,
They ponder their old vine.
"Why must we stand so straight?
The breeze, it can't wait!"

When Branches Bend in Mourning

The branches bow, a comic sight,
As leaves debate their plight.
"Which one of us is best?"
A argument in leafy jest.

"Oh, Mr. Oak, so proud and tall,
You think you know it all!"
But laughing in the shade,
Was a willow who just swayed.

The Lush Embrace of Longing

A vine reached out with all its might,
For sunlight just out of sight.
"Oh dear, I feel so lost!"
Grumbled it, with heavy cost.

The daisies giggled in delight,
While petals waved goodnight.
"Don't stretch so far, you fool!"
"Stay close, you'll be cool!"

Traces of Time on Leafy Pages

Old leaves rustle tales of yore,
Of summers spent and seasons bore.
"Remember when the wind was bold?"
"Or when we danced, so bright and bold?"

But now they sigh, as stories fade,
In shadows where dreams were laid.
"Let's write on new leafy scrolls!"
"Before our time truly rolls!"

The Weight of a Thousand Seasons

In the garden, I do sigh,
Chasing light that passes by.
With a weight that feels so grand,
It seems I'm stuck on this patch of land.

Each breeze brings a wishful grin,
But I'm tangled in my frilly fin.
If only I could sprout some wings,
Oh, the joy that freedom brings!

Ribbons of Resilience

I wear my greens like a fashion show,
Twirling gently, putting on a glow.
Those pesky pests, they munch and bite,
"Munch away!" I say, with all my might.

Though storms may shake my tiny frame,
With humor, I return to the game.
A couple of laughs, a wiggle or two,
My ribbons dance in colors anew!

Secrets in the Soft Moss

Beneath the shade, where whispers dwell,
The moss tells tales, but I can't tell.
It giggles softly as it grows,
A secret party, who really knows?

With mushrooms popping like confetti,
I swear they're plotting, all too petty.
I bend my fronds and eavesdrop low,
"Hey, moss, share a laugh before you go!"

A Lament for Lost Roots

Oh, my roots once deep and wide,
Now it seems they've run to hide.
I search the soil with a puzzled gaze,
"Did you leave me in this maze?"

While others boast of strength and size,
I tell my tales with widened eyes.
"Dig deeper," I giggle, "let's have some fun!
Maybe we'll find them with the morning sun!"

Melancholy of the Forest Floor

In the shadows where ferns do grow,
They whisper tales of woe and low.
Amidst the roots, a tickle creeps,
While mushrooms giggle, the forest sleeps.

Hiding from the sun's bright rays,
They plot their jokes for rainy days.
A squirrel snorts; a rabbit grins,
And leaves are tossed like festive sins.

With every rustle, secrets spill,
As crickets laugh and frogs stand still.
'This is my home!' the ferns declare,
While ants march past without a care.

A Solitary Leaf's Reflection

A leaf lay lost, oh what a plight,
He pondered deep into the night.
'Why can't I dance like those on high?
I'm stuck down here; oh me, oh my!'

His friends above are swirling bright,
While he gets stuck in webs of fright.
'What good is green if you're a bore?
I'll start a band!' he starts to roar.

The vines all chuckle, the twigs all groan,
But one brave branch says, 'You're not alone!'
And so began the leafy cheer,
With laughter growing loud and clear.

Echoes of a Verdant Past

In ancient woods where laughter's lost,
The ferns recount their funny cost.
'Twas not a beast, nor daring knight,
But simply leaves in a wild fight.

'Who took the sun? A bird? A crow?'
'No, just the fog, you silly show!'
The moss rolls eyes, the roots all sigh,
While shadows dance and passers-by.

'Remember when we wore a cap?'
'Oh yes! A stylish, leafy flap!'
Grownups may frown and scold with haste,
But who'd deny a forest taste?

Sighs of the Woodland Breeze

The woodland breeze begins to laugh,
As ferns spin tales of the latest gaffe.
'It's hard to dream with bugs so near,
They nibble bits, then disappear!'

With each soft gust, come silly sighs,
While daisies roll their sleepy eyes.
'Oh, watch that oak, he's losing style,
Don't let the squirrels stick out your smile!'

What blooms today is past tomorrow,
With whispers soft, then bursts of sorrow.
Yet ferns, they giggle in between,
For jest is where the blooms are seen.

Timeless Whispers of the Wild

In the forest, whispers dance,
Leaves gossiping, in a trance.
A squirrel chuckles, high and proud,
While ferns giggle, soft and loud.

Mushrooms winking, quite the show,
Beneath their caps, secrets flow.
The wind makes jokes, puts on a ruse,
A tickle on the ferns' green shoes.

Beneath the sun, they sway and jest,
In nature's clowning, they're the best.
With every rustle, laughter springs,
Oh, what joy this wild life brings!

So come and join the leafy cheer,
In shades of green, all troubles clear.
Let's laugh with nature, let it be,
A festival of glee, you see!

The Shade of Unspoken Sorrows

In the shade, a secret sigh,
Ferns lament, yet still they try.
With drooping fronds, they poke and tease,
Joking with shadows, humbling trees.

A bumblebee makes quite a fuss,
Bumping 'round like it's so us.
The ferns just chuckle, in their shade,
Pretending sorrows, but not afraid.

With every droplet that leaks down,
They wear it well, a leafy crown.
Oh, how they ponder, oh so sly,
With every sigh, they ask, "Oh why?"

But through the laughter and the frowns,
They shimmy sweet in grassy gowns.
For every trouble, jokes arise,
In nature's play, wisdom lies!

Nurtured in Grief's Embrace

In the garden, tears and grins,
Ferns dance lightly, it begins.
A raindrop falls, oh what a plight,
They joke, "Well, we're all wet tonight!"

Through sorrowed roots and playful spritz,
Each leaf a smile, in shadow it flits.
Tickling flowers with softest sighs,
While the moon peeks with sleepy eyes.

Their laughter ebbs with morning light,
As sunbeams snag their dreams at night.
"What's life without a chuckle or two?"
They whisper, "Let the fun ensue!"

So in grief's arms they softly sway,
Finding joy in the bright decay.
For laughter blooms where shadows creep,
In every whisper, wisdom sleeps!

Lament of the Unyielding Green

In the forest, greens do bloom,
Ferns joke about, dispelling gloom.
With every breeze, they share a grin,
Unyielding cheer, where laughs begin.

The dandelions can't help but shout,
"Why pout, dear ferns? Let's dance about!"
Their roots entwined, a bond so clear,
They cheer on life, year after year.

Even when storms come banging loud,
They stand together, brave and proud.
"Let's make a toast to rainy days!"
They cheer and laugh in countless ways.

So here's to greens that never yield,
Finding laughter in every field.
As long as they can sway and play,
In life's mad game, they'll find a way!

Longing Beneath the Shrub's Shade

Beneath the green, I sit and sigh,
A tiny breeze, a feathered spy.
The sun above, it plays a game,
While I just plot my botanical fame.

With roots so fine, I crave a dance,
But dirt's my stage, not chance romance.
I peek at blooms, all bright and bold,
While I just rustle, meek and cold.

A ladybug has stolen my heart,
Yet here I stay, a quiet part.
She flutters by, I stay confined,
Her whispered jokes, so unrefined.

I giggle low, a fateful laugh,
Life's beauty hides in simple craft.
The bush is thick, my dreams are tall,
In shadows cast, I have my ball.

The Memory of Humble Roots

In soil so rich, my humor grows,
With croaking frogs, in careful prose.
I reminisce on roots so wide,
Yet giggle softly, tucked inside.

Oh, how I long to stretch and climb,
To reach the sky, defy all time.
But here I am, short and spry,
A court jester in a leafy tie.

The ants parade in shiny suits,
While I remain, all leafy hoots.
They march with pride, I tease and poke,
Among the greens, I play the joke.

A lesson learned in leaves and fun,
To be a sprout, though dreams weigh a ton.
For laughter blooms in every nook,
And joy is found in nature's book.

A Tale of Shadows and Softness

In cool, soft shade where whispers dwell,
A laughing breeze begins to tell.
The shadows dance with a flicker or two,
While I just sway, a silly view.

I watch the world, all bustling by,
With roots so deep, I ponder why.
These clumsy critters trip and fall,
And I just chuckle, what a brawl.

The sunbeams peek, but I don't mind,
For in my shade, sweet peace I find.
Yet thoughts drift off to blooms up high,
And silly dreams of wings to fly.

So here I sit, a spectator's role,
Watching all, the fun is whole.
Life's but a laugh beneath the leaves,
In shadows soft, where humor weaves.

In the Company of Silence

In quiet nooks, I hoot and laugh,
Creating joy, my secret craft.
With silence loud, I take my time,
For chuckles echo, oh so prime.

A snail slips by, all slimy grace,
While I just giggle, a leafy face.
Oh how I wish to join the spree,
Yet here I sit, a stump of glee.

The total calm is full of fun,
With shadows creeping 'til day is done.
I can't escape my humble fate,
Yet in this stillness, I just wait.

For in the hush, the laughs abound,
In freedom's arms, my glee is found.
Among the greens, I spend my days,
In silence sweet, where humor plays.

Twilight's Gentle Touch

In the garden where shadows play,
Leaves giggle as they sway.
Whispers of twilight, soft and bright,
Embrace the mischief of the night.

Crickets sing in funny tones,
Tickling the air like silly cones.
A breeze snorts through branches grand,
Nature's humor, unplanned and spanned.

Moonbeams dance upon the lawn,
As daisies boast of a prank gone on.
With each glance, the petals tease,
Inviting laughter with such ease.

In twilight's clutch, the world chortles,
While shadows waltz through leafy portals.
Together, they weave a comical tale,
With each rustling leaf, they prevail.

The Dance of Time's Breath

Time jiggles and shakes like a jelly bean,
Ticking away with a giggly sheen.
The clock winks with a cheeky grin,
As each tick-tock brings new whim.

Willows wave their leafy hands,
Chirping tales of distant lands.
Rabbits bounce with a comical flair,
Synchronized steps in the moonlit air.

The grass all chuckles, feeling spry,
While daisies wink at passersby.
Each moment frolics, dances more,
Celebrating time that's never a bore.

In this curious waltz, we find delight,
As laughter twirls into the night.
A playful pirouette, a giggle set free,
In the dance of hours, joyful spree.

An Unheard Symphony of Greens

Among the leaves, a concert stirs,
With gusty laughs and gentle purrs.
The ferns, they wiggle, quite confused,
Wondering why they haven't used.

A saxophone made of snap and crack,
While moths do jazz in their own knack.
Grass chirps loudly, a verdant band,
As colors join to make their stand.

The trees sway high, a silent cheer,
As twigs tap rhythm, loud and clear.
Hidden tones, like secrets shared,
Nature's symphony, none prepared.

In laughter's echo, the night is bold,
Wrinkled smiles as stories unfold.
The greens unite under a moonbeam,
Turning a forest into a dream.

Echoes in the Thicket

In the thicket, whispers curtsy low,
Chuckles bounce where soft winds blow.
With every rustle, a jest ignites,
Making mirth through starry nights.

Brambles crack jokes, teasing the light,
While shadows plot in vivid fright.
A toad, quite proud, hops with a sway,
As the vine-laced jesters join the play.

Crickets scribble notes in the dark,
While fireflies dance with a glowing spark.
Together they weave an echoing tune,
That shimmers like laughter beneath the moon.

As the thicket chuckles in delight,
Each secret shared brings joy to the night.
Nature beams with its playful art,
In every echo, it warms the heart.

Emotions Entwined in Roots

In the forest, I wear a frown,
My leafy friends, they fall down.
A little rain, they sway and swoon,
Yet here I am, stuck like a boon.

The sun shines bright, they twist and tease,
While I stand here, longing for ease.
Do they laugh at my tangled plight?
Oh, how I wish I could take flight!

A squirrel mocks, with a sprightly leap,
While I remain, rooted, and steep.
In humor, sorrow often calls,
Yet I'm the joke, who seldom falls!

So here I stay, with all my quirks,
A jester's role among the works.
Entwined in roots, my heart does dance,
Finding fun in fate's odd chance.

The Absence of Weight in Green

In a patch of grass, I spill my thoughts,
Light as air, my worries are fraught.
With laughter twinkling in the breeze,
Why do the daisies hold such ease?

My fronds feel heavy, a comic blunder,
While roses rise, sweet as thunder.
Are they all plotting to leave me here?
Oh, to be light, without any fear!

The ladybugs giggle, what a sight!
I shimmy and shake, to the left, to the right.
But the weight of my humor pins me down,
In a garden full of joy, I might drown!

Yet amidst my woes, the fun shines through,
With each silly stance, I find a cue.
Absence of weight? I'm a cloud in disguise,
Wondering why I don't float to the skies!

A Journey Unknown Amongst the Shadows

In the twilight, shadows play tricks,
While I plan my moves, what a fix!
Each turn I take feels like a game,
A journey unknown, it's all quite the same.

The mud squelches under my feet,
I trip and tumble, oh, what a feat!
With roots that tangle, I can't be fast,
As silly giggles from grasses are cast.

A firefly flickers, it blinks with glee,
"Come join the dance, dear friend, just be free!"
But here I am, with a timid bow,
Miss the sparkle? Oh, what a cow!

So I embrace this shadowy jest,
Though my legs are tangled, I'll do my best.
For every stumblin' step that I take,
Is a laugh at fate, a fun little wake!

The Shade's Hidden Heartache

In shadows deep where laughter fades,
Ferns wear their joy like old charades.
They gossip green beneath the trees,
Whispering secrets with the breeze.

A rabbit hops, it's quite a show,
Yet ferns just sigh; they steal the glow.
Their fronds all droop; what a disgrace,
In nature's dance, they lose the race.

What is a plant to do for fun,
When sunlight plays, and they can't run?
They stretch and twist in leafy woe,
Poking fun at the sun's warm glow.

Yet shadowy friends, they still unite;
In verdant corners, they delight.
A band of greens with dreams to throw,
Behind their backs, they'll put on a show.

Secrets of the Shaded Grove

In the grove, where shadows dance,
Ferns tell tales of lost romance.
A beetle scurries, a leaf does sway,
While ferns roll eyes in their green ballet.

Chirps of crickets fill the air,
But ferns just sulk; they don't quite care.
They envy blooms who flaunt and sway,
While in the shade, they drearily stay.

An owl hoots, it starts to tease,
"Come join the fun; please do, if you please!"
But ferns just shrug, "What's there to be?
We're masters of hidden misery."

Yet in their hearts, a laugh will grow,
For every breeze brings tales to sow.
The secrets shared in laughter's pour,
Make ferns the kings of shaded lore.

Beneath Leafy Veils of Regret

Beneath the leaves where ferns convene,
They wring their fronds in dismal sheen.
"Oh, to bask in the sun's embrace!
Instead, we hide; what a dreary place!"

Their neighbor, an oak, is grand and proud,
While ferns just blend in with the crowd.
"Is it too late for a second chance?
Perhaps we'll join the sunlight dance!"

Yet through the whispers of the night,
They chuckle softly at their plight.
"Why climb so high or strive to race?
We thrive in shade, and we've got grace!"

So with a laugh, they lift their fronds,
Plotting escapes to sunlit ponds.
Beneath their leafy veils so bright,
They embrace their shade with sheer delight.

Nature's Quiet Elegy

Nature hums a gentle tune,
While ferns lament beneath the moon.
With every breeze, they sigh so deep,
"Why must we all just sit and weep?"

A squirrel scampers, a bird takes flight,
But ferns just plot through day and night.
"Who needs the sun? We're fine right here!
Just us and shadows—what a cheer!"

In silent corners, they exchange a grin,
Their leafy hearts, a riot within.
While misty mornings mask their fun,
They chuckle softly at the sun.

And deep within their shaded throng,
They sing a quiet, leafy song.
With every twist and every sway,
Ferns find their joy in a funny way.

Ferns Under the Gaze of Stars

Underneath the twinkling sky,
Ferns gather for a giggly sigh.
They gossip about the moon's bright face,
And debate who has the best lace.

One claims her fronds catch every light,
While another just loves hiding at night.
With whispers swirling, tales take flight,
While crickets just laugh at their delight.

They sway in rhythm, a dance so weird,
A leafy parody that's much too cheered.
Stars above can't help but blink,
As ferns share secrets over a drink.

So if you wander 'neath the starlit beams,
Listen closely and join their dreams.
The ferns may jest, but they're wise, it's true,
In the world of greens, they're the comedic crew.

Nostalgia of the Woodland Floor

Upon the forest's cozy bed,
Ferns reminisce with a giggly thread.
They tell stories of mushrooms from afar,
And elephant trees who once were stars.

A mossy carpet joins in the fun,
Rolling about, chasing the sun.
They laugh at the squirrels with acorn hats,
And share tales of dancing, oh, imagine that!

With every breeze, the memories swirl,
Ferns whisper soft in a leafy whirl.
If trees could chuckle, they'd join the spree,
As the forest giggles in timeless glee.

Each shadow a memory, light-as-a-feather,
Collecting tales shared in sunny weather.
For in these woods, where whispers soar,
Nostalgic greens yearn to explore.

Gentle Holds of the Hidden World

In shadows deep and corners shy,
Ferns hold secrets, oh my, oh my!
They whisper soft when no one's near,
A tickle of laughter, a sprinkle of cheer.

They cradle the wild in a leafy embrace,
Inside their folds, a cozy place.
With twirls and sways, they tell a tale,
Of adventures that slide like a ship's white sail.

Hidden worlds beneath sunshine bright,
Ferns speak in green, a dazzling sight.
They nudge the shy with a gentle tease,
Encouraging giggles on the woodland breeze.

From root to tip, their stories unfold,
In whispered tones, oh so bold.
Join in their laughter, let worries unfurl,
In the arms of ferns, find the hidden swirl.

The Unspoken Words of a Leaf

The leaves know much, but seldom chat,
Especially when the wind is fat.
They hang out together, in quiet grace,
Swapping jokes with a serious face.

One leaf said, 'Do I look more round?',
While another took pride in being unbound.
With every rustle, a laugh or two,
They jest like friends who just broke through.

As flowers bloom, leaves roll their eyes,
'It's not that easy to be so wise!'
Yet in the silence, they truly shine,
Sharing whispers that feel divine.

With roots in the ground and dreams up high,
These leafy jesters quietly pry.
In the forest's nook, their humor weaves,
Around the tales that a leaf believes.

The Quiet Struggle of the Undergrowth

In the shadows where ferns reside,
Hiding secrets they cannot confide.
With leaves all a-quiver, they giggle with glee,
Hoping the sunlight won't spot them, you see.

The worms tell a tale of their hidden delight,
As bugs buzz along in a fluttering flight.
The world above laughs, but they don't seem to care,
They're dancing in silence, with style to spare.

In the dark where they grumble, they'd trade for a sun,
Yet laugh at the fact they're not out for fun.
With roots deep in mischief, they plot and they scheme,
A jolly brigade in their underleaf dream.

So up with your shovels, all gardeners near!
These leafy comedians bring laughter, not fear.
Join in their chorus, the soil is a stage,
For ferns in their frolics, all leafy and sage.

When Shadows Dance with Sorrow

In moonlit shadows, they start a parade,
Ferns flailing wildly, a leafy charade.
With whispers of giggles they sway to the beat,
Though missing the sun, they dance in the heat.

But oh, how they ponder on fortune's cruel fate,
Watching the daisies and tulips sedate.
They sigh with a rustle, a comedic lament,
While clinging to roots that are time-spent and bent.

As shadows dive deeper, the fun starts to shift,
With prancing and bouncing, they share a good lift.
A raucous ensemble, through laughter they weave,
Amidst the dark whispers, they won't take their leave.

So in the dark, a festival brews,
Beneath pines and oaks, they'll share their old blues.
Ferns waltz through the gloom, undeterred by the plight,
For sorrow's just shadow, and they'll dance through the night.

A Frond's Broken Promise

Promised a skyward, luxurious view,
But ended up tangled in grass with a boo.
A frond took a gamble, oh what a mistake,
Now curls up in shame, saying, "Where's all the cake?"

With dreams of a feature, a starlit reward,
Now grounded and giggly, feeling ignored.
"I'm supposed to be grand!" cried the leaf in despair,
While critters around let out loud hallelujahs in air.

Yet joy is a trickster, a fun little sprite,
And soon enough, laughter turns wrongs into right.
The old frond then chuckles, "I'm happy with friends,
For they make the wild way less lonely, and bends."

So here's to the journeys that take an odd turn,
Where broken old fronds can still twist and still yearn.
For life is a jest, and with laughter we play,
In tangled commitments, we find joy every day.

The Heartbeat of the Hidden

Beneath the green cover, a heartbeat so sly,
Ferns chuckle and whisper as days drift by.
They tease with their secrets, in rustles and sways,
Mocking the rays in their sunniest phase.

A riot of colors they insist on suppressing,
As joyfully verdant, their humor's confessing.
While petals above flaunt their beauty with pride,
The ferns wear their laughter like nature's fun guide.

With whispers of shadows and laughter as might,
They plot their next dance when the moon's shining bright.
Their roots stretch for miles, a sly raucous crew,
Turning the forest floor into comedy's zoo.

So next time you wander through thicket and grime,
Listen close to the ferns—it's humor they rhyme.
In the quietest places, where not many tread,
Lies laughter and joy that no one has read.

Cultivating Silence

In the garden, whispers play,
Leaves chuckle, swaying gay.
Sunlight giggles through the trees,
Grass tickles toes, with gentle breeze.

Frogs croak jokes from their perch,
While insects dance, in joyful search.
Oh, the secrets that they keep,
In the quiet, laughter's leap.

Roots hold tales, beneath the ground,
Where the goofy gnomes are found.
With shovels made of candy canes,
They dig for humor, not for gains.

So hush, my friend, and take a seat,
In this funny world, so sweet.
Listen close, let silence bloom,
In every corner, joy takes room.

The Soft Murmur of Green

In leafy halls, where giggles grow,
Squirrels boast of acorn hoes.
Mossy carpets, a perfect prank,
Where laughter hides in every bank.

The flowers wink, with colors bright,
Bees wear crowns, hold court in flight.
While ladybugs with spots of cheer,
Spin silly tales for all to hear.

The gentle breeze, a whispering tease,
Dances through branches with utmost ease.
Oh, the green holds a merry sound,
In every laugh, nature's round.

So join the frolic, don't be shy,
Where the ticklish ivy seems to sigh.
In this soft murmur, find your play,
With jokes of dirt and leaves on display.

Dreams Within the Dew

Droplets gather like cheeky sprites,
Whispering dreams of funny sights.
Each tiny bead, a secret wish,
For playful frogs and dancing fish.

In the early morning light,
Caterpillars wear hats so bright.
Ants parade with pomp and flair,
A buzzing chorus fills the air.

Through the grass, a tickle shimmers,
While fairies laugh, their glow just glimmers.
As petals blush, the jokes unfold,
In dew-kissed realms of stories told.

So sip the dawn, let humor flow,
In nature's jest, we find our glow.
Each droplet carries laughter's cue,
In dreams we weave, with morning dew.

The Edge of Ferny Whispers

At the borders where fronds sway,
Secrets mingle in bright display.
Whispers echo on the breeze,
Telling tales with utmost ease.

Critters gather for the show,
Mice in tuxedos, ready to go.
The overlord of laughter sits,
A plucky rabbit, throwing fits.

The ferns sway with giggling grace,
As nature teases every space.
With shadows dancing, plays unfold,
In this green realm, the boldest told.

So trudge along, embrace the jest,
In ferny whispers, find your rest.
Each chuckle, a step, a twirl,
In laughter's arms, let's all unfurl.

Ephemeral Elegance

In the garden, fronds do sway,
A dance so light, they steal the day.
Sassy leaves in a breezy twirl,
Who knew greens could cause such a whirl?

With sunlight, they pose, full of glee,
Shimmering bright for all to see.
Yet when the clouds begin to brood,
They sulk in shadows, quite in the mood.

A spin here, a flip there, no one can tell,
How a fern can live its life so well.
With whispers of wind and laughs of the breeze,
It sprouts up dreams with such charming ease.

But when the rains come pouring down,
They frown just like a wilting clown.
In pouting greens, they murmur and croak,
While the daisies laugh, as if it's a joke.

Shade's Hesitant Truth

In the cool dark, ferns stand shy,
Peeking out, but oh so sly.
Their rustling secrets, a giggly spree,
Eavesdropping on the buzzing bee.

With wavy arms and a twinkle bright,
They stretch for sun, but fear the light.
What a drama, oh what a jest,
In hidden plots, they comfort the rest.

When shadows whisper, they laugh on cue,
A comic show, just for a few.
Yet they cringe, oh the sun's cruel glare,
A paradox wrapped in green affair.

They tilt and lean, like they've had too much,
Trying to blend, in a hush-hush crutch.
With spindly grace, and a flip of a leaf,
They dance to the tune of leafy grief.

Remnants of a Shaded Journey

In the woods, where shadows play,
Ferns linger long, in a whimsical way.
With every rustle, tales they weave,
Of awkward moments, we can't believe.

They trip on roots and tumble down,
Emerging green, yet looking like a clown.
A twirl in the dusk, a flop in the glade,
Who said a fern can't be a charade?

Underneath skies, so gray and blue,
They share their worries, as good friends do.
But when the sun peeks, oh what a sight,
They scramble to hide, fearing the light.

With every sigh, they giggle then hide,
Their leafy antics, they can't abide.
Amidst their charm, they'll always remain,
The jesters of nature, with laughs and disdain.

In the Cool Embrace of Shadows

Beneath arches where shadows sigh,
Ferns shake their fronds, oh me, oh my!
With every breeze, a playful tease,
In leafy laughter, they sway with ease.

Huddled close, they share a plot,
Where sunlight's harshness, they've all forgot.
A tangle of jokes in a green cocoon,
The night's soft giggle, a velvet tune.

As moonlight dances, they sway and bend,
In secrets shared, they find a friend.
Sprouting tales of wandering hearts,
In shadows' embrace, where laughter starts.

Yet drops of rain bring a dramatic flair,
They shudder and creak, as if in despair.
But come the dawn, with a sunny wink,
They giggle alive, ready to blink.

A Silent Cry Amongst the Greens

In the shade where green things sigh,
Leaves whisper secrets, oh my,
A chuckle escapes from roots so stout,
"Why's no one watering us out?"

Amongst the ferns, a giggle grows,
Tickled by breezes, they strike poses,
"Did you hear the tree snore last night?"
"Yes, and it shook the bugs in fright!"

Petals nodding, in jest they tease,
"Can you dance, or do you freeze?"
"I can sway, but not for long,
Entranced by nature's silly song!"

In the greens, the laughter lingers,
With each rustle of winded fingers,
"Let's serve the sun a cup of shade,
And giggle while the sunlight's made!"

The Fragile Dance of Time

Beneath the swaying, leafy veil,
The shadows tell a silly tale,
Of trembling stems that twist and twirl,
As insects join the crazy whirl!

Time teases with a comical grin,
"Who'll be first to dance and spin?"
A beetle laughs, it takes the lead,
While clovers cheer, no time to heed!

"Oh dear!" the daisies start to roar,
"Did that earthworm just drop and snore?"
The brook giggles, runs in glee,
As time just winks, "It's all just me!"

Each moment passes, soft, serene,
Yet laughter fills the foliage green,
In this fragile, funny time dance,
Every leaf waits for a chance!

Beneath the Ancient Boughs

Under branches, time whispers low,
While cicadas put on quite a show,
"Hey Acorn, what's your game today?"
"I'm aiming for a tree's buffet!"

The roots begin a raucous chat,
"Do you think I'm just a mat?"
A squirrel scoffs, "It's quite absurd,
You're a home, not just a word!"

The trunk winks, with stories grand,
"Want to hear about my band?"
"Just woodpeckers and a frog,"
"Quirky singers on this bog!"

Beneath such boughs, absurdly bright,
Nature dances through day and night,
So come, my friend, let's laugh and play,
With every bloom that brightens the day!

Sprouts of Forgotten Echoes

In the meadow, whispers wind,
"Did the daisies just grin?"
With petals brimming cheer so bright,
They nod and say, "Yes, what a sight!"

A dandelion makes a fuss,
"I puff my seeds, you miss your bus!"
"Careful now, you might just sprout!"
"In that case, I'm all about!"

The grass giggles beneath our feet,
"Can you hear that tune? It's sweet!"
A frog leaps in with rhythm fine,
"Hop along, it's party time!"

So here we are in silly jest,
Among the blooms, we feel so blessed,
Echoes of laughter fill the air,
In nature's arms, without a care!

The Pause of Nature's Breath

In the garden, I stand still,
Waiting for a squirrel's thrill.
A moment brief, then gone in haste,
Nature's pause is never waste.

Sunshine teases through the trees,
A breeze whispers like a sneeze.
I'm wondering if this is fate,
Or just a bug who can't wait.

Flowers giggle, insects hum,
Yet here I am, looking numb.
The world spins in a jolly dance,
While I just miss my chance.

Nature chuckles, can't you see?
Leafy friends wink back at me.
Oh what joy, a silly sight,
Just pause and laugh in delight!

Lost in the Lattice of Life

Among the vines and leafy sheets,
I stumble on my own two feet.
A twist here, a turn with flair,
Oh dear me, I'm lost somewhere!

The raindrops giggle as they fall,
I can't keep track, oh what a brawl!
Nature's maze, a playful trick,
I'm the punchline of the flick.

Every turn brings forth a grin,
"To lose oneself? Where to begin?"
The flowers wave, "You'll find your way!"
As I trip over roots at play.

But through the laughs, I surely learn,
Life's a dance, a wiggle and turn.
In shades and scents, I'll find my tune,
Amongst the laughter of the moon!

A Soliloquy of Shade

Beneath the tree's wide canopy,
I muse aloud, "Why are there three?"
The shadows laugh and whisper tales,
Of sunny days and silly fails.

A squirrel juggles acorns high,
While I just sit and wonder why.
Life's a circus, don't you see?
With leafy witnesses, just like me!

The sun peeks down, a prankster bold,
Tickling my toes, a sight to behold.
"Stay still, my friend!" I shout in jest,
But the shade just chuckles, "You need a rest."

So here I lounge, the world a show,
With leafy friends and banter flow.
In nature's stage, where I belong,
A soliloquy, a laugh-filled song!

Dreams Woven in Leaves

In a world where dreams take flight,
Leaves whisper secrets, oh so light.
With every rustle comes a cheer,
"Come join the fun!" they seem to jeer.

The winds stretch wide, a silly tease,
I scramble to chase after these.
In realms where laughter fills the air,
Even dreams are light as fare.

A twig bends low, a playful bow,
And all around, my heart takes how!
Nature's comedy, always grand,
Where nothing's serious, just a band.

As slumber kisses, gently weave,
In leafy dreams, I'll never grieve.
For every chuckle that I hear,
Makes this life a dance, my dear!

Nature's Heartbeat in the Shadows

In the woods where shadows play,
A squirrel jokes about the day.
Leaves giggle as they dance on air,
Whispers of secrets everywhere.

The moon chuckles, peeking down,
At twinkling stars in fluffy gown.
Bugs debate in tiny teams,
Swapping tales of moonlit dreams.

Mushrooms wear their rainbow hats,
While snails race in slow-poke spats.
Nature's laughter, soft and clear,
Tickles the heart, brings great cheer.

In shadows deep where jokes are born,
The forest laughs from dusk till morn.
Gathered titter, rustling fun,
Nature's heartbeat, never done.

In the Quietude of the Wild

In the still where silence reigns,
A wise old owl complains and wanes.
"Why do crickets always sing?
Don't they feel the time they bring?"

But flowers grin with colors bright,
"Gossip's our game, we spread delight!"
Trees chuckle as they sway and bend,
Saying, "Nature's humor has no end."

A raccoon, dressed in shades of night,
Scampers by, claims he's quite a sight.
"Look at me! I'm stylish and spry!"
He shimmies, as fireflies fly by.

With every rustle and soft sigh,
The wild's whispers make us laugh and cry.
A symphony of jest and cheer,
In nature's arms, we hold it dear.

Ruminations Amongst the Leafy Thicket

Beneath the leaves where secrets hide,
Caterpillars dream of a towering glide.
"Maybe I'll dance," one sings with glee,
"First catch me if you can, oh wee!"

Frogs chuckle near the bubbling brook,
"Who needs a game? Let's write a book!"
They scribble rhymes on lily pads,
Finding joy in their playful fads.

Ants parade with tiny feet,
Marching off to a rhythm beat.
"Join us, quick! The party's right here!"
Says one, waving all without fear.

In this thicket of leafy chats,
The humor's endless, just like hats.
With laughter ringing through the trees,
The wild's a stage, come join with ease.

When Time Turns to Leaves

When time turns leaves in swirling dance,
The wind giggles, taking a chance.
"Catch me if you can!" it sings,
As branches sway like playful swings.

Dandelions puff with pride,
"Watch us float, we're no ones' guide!"
They tumble gently, drifting far,
A cloud parade, a twinkling star.

Bees buzz about, always in a rush,
"Doing what? Oh, just a big hush!"
They sip the nectar, sweet delight,
Making the meadow their party night.

As the season teases time away,
Nature laughs in a merry sway.
In every rustle, laughter gleans,
Time turns leaves, through all it means.

Solace in the Silent Glade

In the glade where shadows play,
The leaves wiggle, come what may.
A squirrel dances, quite absurd,
Chasing whispers, never heard.

With sticks as swords, the critters cheer,
They duel with joy, erase the fear.
Laughter echoes, soft and sweet,
In this realm, they skip, they fleet.

Sunbeams tickle every nook,
While giggles rise like a storybook.
Nature's jesters, full of glee,
In their world, so wild and free.

Yet come the night, the shadows creep,
And all the funbirds fall asleep.
In dreams they dance, in dreams they play,
Until the sun brings a new day.

In the Depths of the Green Abyss

Deep within the leafy maze,
A forgotten shoe, left in a daze.
A raccoon laughs, what a sight!
He wears it proudly, a fashion blight.

The frogs are crooning in a band,
With twigs and leaves, a wild strand.
They drum on logs, they sing out loud,
In this green abyss, they're feeling proud.

A curious snail joins the show,
With sequined shells, a superstar glow.
While fireflies flicker, twinkle, and twirl,
In the depths, it's a crazy whirl.

Yet when dawn beams its golden light,
The party ends, oh what a fright!
The critters yawn and take their rest,
Awaiting nightfall, the wildest fest.

Tales of the Unseen Heart

In the thicket where secrets dwell,
A shy little mouse weaves a spell.
He whispers tales of cheese and wine,
And under the moon, his stories shine.

With a wink, he glances around,
But the hedgehog snores, deep on the ground.
He flips through dreams of grand repas,
As if a feast could bring him class.

An owl chuckles at moonlit sights,
As the beavers sway, enjoying the nights.
They build a dam with topsy glee,
Crafting wonders for all to see.

But when dawn breaks, quiet returns,
With a soft sigh, the heart churns.
The tales still echo in the brisk air,
As all creatures dream with a flair.

Beneath the Canopy of Melancholy

Underneath the droopy leaves,
A turtle sighs, as if he grieves.
He wears a frown, a heavy shell,
While dragonflies buzz their gossip well.

The ants march on with tiny hats,
Holding meetings, bumping bats.
What's the problem? Who can say?
In the gloom, they dance and play.

The clouds above are in dismay,
"Should we bring rain?" they softly sway.
But a shout from the grass breaks the funk,
A cricket croons, bringing up the junk!

And as the sun peeks through the gloom,
All creatures wiggle, banishing doom.
With laughter rising from the heart,
Life beneath the trees restarts!

Beneath the Cloak of Green

In shadows deep, the critters play,
A cabbage patch holds a grand buffet.
The whispers laugh, the daisies tease,
While ferns observe with silent ease.

They roll their eyes at the buzzing flies,
And pine for gossip of the butterfly.
As sunlight dances through the trees,
They sigh, "Oh, to blend with some cheese!"

The wind comes in with a puff and a flair,
Declaring it's time to style hair with care.
The branches sway, a leafy disco,
But ferns just cringe, feeling the woe.

In leafy cloaks, they dream and dream,
Of running wild, a ferny team.
Yet stuck they are, in one small grove,
Pretending to be grand when they're not so bold.

A Leaf's Lament to the Sky

Oh sky so blue, with clouds so white,
You swoosh and swirl, a perfect sight.
While I'm here stuck, in one sad shade,
Desiring bright, yet slowly fade.

I wave my fronds, a plea so spry,
To dance up high, to float and fly.
The birds just giggle, flapping their wings,
While I near sob, my heartstrings sing.

If I could twirl with a sunset's glance,
Instead of longing, I'd chance a dance.
But here I stand, a sad green heap,
With all my dreams buried, buried deep.

One day I'll have my moment, surprise!
And shimmer bright up in those skies.
Till then I'll hold my leafy brew,
A secret wish, just between me and you.

The Forgotten Language of the Woods

In woods where whispers once held sway,
Now critters chat in a different way.
The flowers gossip, the mushrooms nod,
While ferns roll thoughts, feeling quite odd.

"Oh dear," said one, "I miss the old days,
When trees would dance and the breeze would haze."
But ferns just fluttered, feeling quite shy,
"For we're just ferns—no wings to fly."

They envy roots that grasp the ground,
While leaves above twirl all around.
In cast-off jokes of nature's play,
Ferns twitch in silence, dismayed and gray.

With every rustle, a joke lost in vain,
A punchline buried in the earthy lane.
Yet still they chuckle, in their own domain,
"Perhaps it's best we just stay plain!"

Solitude Etched in Green

In solitude, I sway and bend,
With thoughts so weird, they never end.
The squirrels scamper, the rabbits hop,
While I just stand, a quiet prop.

They talk and chatter, a lively crew,
While I'm the wallflower, painted in dew.
Oh to join in with fuzzy friends,
But alas, I'm where the ferniness ends.

My stories curl like wisps of smoke,
In rustling lines, a silent poke.
"Hey there, leaf! Or are you a snack?"
I blush a shade of green, "Oh, cut me some slack!"

Yet here I sway, in my own little place,
Wishing for friends, or just a sweet face.
But for now, I stand tall and proud,
In solitude etched, beneath the cloud.

Embrace of the Forgotten Fronds

In the wood where fronds do sigh,
A dancing shadow flutters by.
It trips on roots and starts to laugh,
Embracing life, a leafy staff.

With curls so wild, they tease the breeze,
Giggling softly among the trees.
A bow to moss and wink to sun,
Fronds retail fun and never shun.

The whispers here, a gentle jest,
A nature's play, a leafy fest.
In every twist, a laughter runs,
While silent trees give nods and puns.

With every rustle, tales unfold,
Of silly things that leaves have told.
Among the roots, they'll weave and spin,
For life's rich humor lies within.

Soft Spoken in the Thickets

In thickets dense, the chatter hums,
Of soft-spoken leaves and gentle drums.
They giggle sweetly in the shade,
A secret dance, a light parade.

Whispers twirl like butterflies,
Mossy jokes that lift the sighs.
Beneath their caps, the sunbeams play,
Tickling petals in a bright ballet.

They swap their tales of sprightful tricks,
As shadows wiggle and sunlight flicks.
In whispers soft, they tease the air,
A hush of giggles everywhere.

So raise a toast to vines unseen,
With laughter sprouting in between.
In every branch, a jest weave tight,
As thickets bloom, all feels just right.

A Reverie Among the Green

A wandering thought beneath a leaf,
Plays hide and seek, a cheeky thief.
In emerald realms, where laughter's born,
Fronds unite, all mischief sworn.

They plot and plan with roots in tow,
In giddy lines, their antics flow.
A prank on petals, a leaf of jest,
A reverie where humor's best.

Tickling soil with a leafy giggle,
As sunshine shines, they start to wriggle.
In whispers, sways, the joy extends,
In every shade, the laughter bends.

So join the fray, don leafy crowns,
Dance with the hues of vibrant towns.
With every rustle, the day shall gleam,
In this green world, we dare to dream.

The Inward Gaze of Leaves

Leaves glance inwards, oh what a sight,
Reflecting laughter in morning light.
They giggle softly, a secret kept,
In green retreats, where dreams have leapt.

With every sway, an inside joke,
A puffing breeze begins to poke.
They smirk at clouds, so high and grand,
And chuckle 'bout the shifting sand.

The world unfolds in leafy charm,
With every twist, a playful arm.
So let us join, in leafy embrace,
And share the joy of this green space.

In inward gaze, we'll find delight,
Among the leaves, our spirits light.
So if you frown, just look around,
For laughter blooms where greens abound.

Elegy of the Emerald Leaf

In the garden's cozy nook,
Where ferns like gossip gather round,
They whisper tales of heartbreak,
While leaves sway softly to the sound.

The squirrels scoff, they roll their eyes,
At such melodrama, oh so bold!
They play with acorns, giggle, tease,
While ferns spin yarns of love retold.

Amidst their fronds, they sigh and pout,
A love that's wilted, oh so true!
But who could love a plant, no doubt,
With roots that cling like skyward glue?

Yet still they dance in evening light,
With shadows bold, a bright surprise.
With rustling sounds, they take flight,
In leafy gowns, and sparkling eyes.

Beneath the Velvet Shade

Beneath the leaves, a secret pact,
Among the fronds, a merry band,
They plan to plot, with whispered act,
To prank the blooms, just as they planned.

'Who needs romance?' the ferns declare,
'When we have shade and fun to share.'
With stems held high, they laugh and play,
In laughing tones, they chase the day.

They mock the daisies, soft and sweet,
And twirl around, in shadows deep,
'Come join our game, don't take a seat,
For love is just a rootless creep!'

Yet even in their teasing ways,
When clouds drift by and sunlight fades,
A hint of wistful charm conveys,
The gentle heart that nature sways.

Green Remembrances

In laughter loud, the ferns unite,
To share their tales of woe and cheer,
One claims a bug had stolen flight,
While others hush, in hushed veneer.

With leafy hands, they hold their sides,
As stories twist and turn about,
A gnome once sat, they now reside,
And sought the blooms with rotund route.

A snail was caught in leafy tales,
Of bitter love and sappy trails,
Yet here beneath the sun's embrace,
They frolic free, a leafy grace.

So let us cheer, for greens remain,
In whisper soft, their joys explain,
While petals turn and roots entwine,
In jestful green, the world seems fine.

Dances in the Dappled Light

In sunlight's edge, the ferns do sway,
With giggles soft and playful leaps,
'Twas not a breeze, but laughter's play,
A foxtrot here, where shadows creep.

The flowers blink, with jealous pride,
As ferns put on their dance parade,
With pirouettes, they hop and glide,
While petals pout in hues of jade.

A toadstool cheerleader yells,
'Come join the fun, you flowery types!'
Yet buds just blush, as laughter swells,
With leafy limbs and leafy wipes.

And as the dusk wraps round the grove,
The ferns will twirl till twilight's close,
For even plants need room to rove,
And find their steps in evening's prose.

Whispers of the Woodland's Sorrow

In the shade where shadows creep,
The ferns gather, secrets to keep.
They chuckle at the squirrel's plight,
As he fumbles nuts—oh, what a sight!

With bristly fronds and crooked fronds,
They share tall tales of mossy ponds.
"Once I danced like the breeze in May,
But now I'm stuck here, come what may!"

A beetle strolls, adorned in style,
He takes a bow, but can't go a mile.
The ferns just giggle, laying low,
"This woodland life is quite the show!"

Through rustling leaves, their laughter flies,
Amidst the trees and painted skies.
They know their quirks, their lives a joke,
In nature's play, they're the punchline folk!

Green Veils of Forgotten Dreams

In a patch where sunlight plays,
The ferns recall their youthful days.
"Oh, remember when we swayed in lines?"
Now we're all just awkward vines!

"Once I tickled a passing bee,
But now I hide—oh woe is me!
My cousins flaunt their vibrant flair,
While I'm just stuck in this damp chair!"

An acorn drops; it clanks with dread,
The ferns just giggle in their bed.
"Do we grow again, or is this fate?
I swear I saw my best mate state!"

With limbs so lush, they dance along,
But feel quite out of step—oh, wrong!
Yet in their greens, there's humor loud,
They're the life of this leafy crowd!

Echoes Underneath the Canopy

Beneath the trees where shadows blend,
The ferns weave tales of every trend.
"Oh, remember when we sought the sun?"
Now we're hiding; this isn't fun!

A snail, the slowest of the crew,
Wanders by, not a thing to do.
"Move it on!" the ferns all shout,
His lethargy makes them pout!

Among the roots, they share their fears,
A clumsy worm just trips and clears.
"We're flexing leaves, he's flexing fate,
So shall we dance, or just berate?"

Yet in their hearts, there's joy so pure,
Making light of what they endure.
A chuckle here, a giggle there,
Their woodland woes simply declare!

A Frond's Silent Grief

In a hush where the sunlight gleams,
The fronds weave in whimsical dreams.
"Oh, the days when we were grand,
Now we're trampled, ain't life bland?"

A tiny robin lands with style,
"What's wrong, green friends? Been in denial?"
The fronds respond with leafy glee,
"Come join our happy misery!"

The wind whispers jokes, quite absurd,
While the ferns pretend not to have heard.
"Once upon a time, I flew!"
Now just rooted, what's a frond to do?

Though days be short and nights be long,
The ferns find humor in every wrong.
Their laughter echoes, light as air,
In the tapestry of life, they share!

Footsteps of an Autumn Wind

The leaves do twirl and twist around,
Like playful sprites that dance unbound.
A gusty chuckle fills the air,
As squirrels jump without a care.

With every crunch beneath my feet,
The ground's a symphony, so sweet.
The wind whispers a silly tale,
Of wandering gnomes with hearts so frail.

Pine cones tumble down like clowns,
While acorns share their silly frowns.
Birds chirp jokes from lofty high,
As branches sway and wink an eye.

In this parade of laughter bright,
Nature's jesters bring delight.
With every step, the world's a stage,
Where autumn plays the jester's page.

Memories Whittled by Rain

Droplets tap, a playful tune,
As puddles form beneath the moon.
A squirrel looks for shelter near,
With thoughts of acorns, oh so dear.

Umbrellas bob like mushrooms sprout,
While people dance, spin about.
Each raindrop laughs, a tickling thing,
As they chase clouds and clouds take wing.

Leaves gather secrets, soft and sly,
While echoes of laughter float on high.
With muddy shoes, we'll race the streams,
And splash in joy, forgetting dreams.

So let the rain come tumbling down,
It's nature's jest, a playful crown.
In squishy socks, we'll not complain,
For joy's often found in the rain!

Resilience Wrapped in Earth

Beneath the soil, the whispers twine,
Resilient roots in secret dine.
They chuckle softly, share their tales,
Of storms they braved, of winds that wail.

Strange seeds sprout with giggling glee,
A dandelion winks at me.
The past can't hold them down, it seems,
They rise up high, like childhood dreams.

Each pebble's laugh, a cheerful sound,
As life finds ways to spin around.
With every sprout, there's mischief spread,
And laughter rustles where they tread.

So cheer for life, in all its quirks,
With nature's humor, joy still lurks.
Through wiggles, jiggles, in the dirt,
Resilience shines, with laughs unshurt.

Where the Quiet Ferns Repose

In shadows deep where soft ferns hide,
The whispers of giggles softly glide.
They sway with grace, a charming sight,
In hush of leaves, they twinkle bright.

Beneath the fronds, a secret plays,
Where mushrooms chuckle through their days.
They tell of tales, of sunlit beams,
And share the joy of woodland dreams.

A rabbit hops, a grin so wide,
His ears flop with every stride.
Amongst the ferns, he's quite the clown,
In nature's realm, he wears the crown.

So in this place where quiet reigns,
The ferns invite us to their games.
In laughter echoing through the trees,
We find the joy, the gentle tease.

The Forest's Unheard Cry

In the woods where shadows tease,
The trees whisper jokes on the breeze.
A squirrel giggles, a rabbit snorts,
As the mushrooms play card games in sports.

Leaves rustle with laughter, oh so spry,
A chorus of chuckles fills the sky.
But the old oak stands grumpy and grey,
Wishing it could join in the play.

The brook joins in with a bubbly tune,
While stones chuckle under the moon.
The forest is wild, but it takes a break,
When the pine trees snore, for goodness' sake!

So gather round, oh leafy mates,
Let's celebrate the funny states.
For even in silence, we won't forget,
Nature's humor is the best bet.

Green Shadows and Silent Nights

In the hush of night, shadows dance,
A raccoon sneaks by, quick in its prance.
With twinkling eyes, it ponders a joke,
While the wise old owl just sits and croaks.

Mossy carpets roll out like great beds,
As fireflies giggle above our heads.
Whispers of laughter fill the air,
Even the crickets can't help but share.

A beetle slicks up in a bright bow tie,
Says, "Life is a party, oh, why so shy?"
With every rustle and little peep,
The forest's secrets are ours to keep.

So raise a glass of dew, my friends,
Let's toast to laughter that never ends.
In shadows of green, we find delight,
Funny whispers in the quiet night.

Elegy of the Dappled Light

Beneath the boughs where sunlight streams,
The daisies dance with hopes and dreams.
A butterfly whispers, "Life's a jest!"
While ladybugs play tag, feeling blessed.

In a patch of dappled light they bide,
Where sunbeams tickle and do not hide.
"Why so serious?" asks the busy bee,
As it buzzes around, so carefree.

The brook chuckles, "I've got the scoop,
On even the oldest, grumpiest troupe!"
While ferns sway lightly in the breeze,
Sharing stories that make the ants wheeze.

So let's compose a merry tune,
Under the watch of the smiling moon.
For in the light of nature's grace,
Laughter teaches us to embrace.

Ferns Weep in Solitude

In the shade, where all is still,
A fern sighs softly, trying to chill.
"Why so lonely?" asks the nearby pine,
"I thought that solitude would be divine!"

But other ferns chime in with cheer,
"We've got our jests, come lend an ear!"
They tickle roots with whispered glee,
Relishing in jibes quite carefree.

The sunbeams poke through leaves above,
Sprinkling laughter like a treasure trove.
"Let's play a game of hide and seek,
For even shadows like to sneak!"

So in their cloistered, leafy nook,
They turn teardrops to laughter—just take a look!
For in the realm where moss does creep,
Ferns find joy in friends, not regret to keep.

www.ingramcontent.com/pod-product-compliance
Lightning Source LLC
Chambersburg PA
CBHW072220070526
44585CB00015B/1424